Nordic Walking

The Beginners Guide To Nordic Pole Walking For Health, Fitness & Adventure

1st Edition

By Desmond Ogley

Table of Contents

Introduction

I want to thank you and congratulate you for purchasing the book, *"Nordic Walking: The Beginners Guide To Nordic Pole Walking For Health, Fitness & Adventure"*.

This book contains proven steps and strategies on how to understand the basics of Nordic walking – what it is all about and what you can do to get the most out of it.

This book gives you a glimpse of where the idea came from. It also includes the basic tutorials about the equipment needed, walking techniques and different pathways and routes where you can perform the activity.

This aims to open your eyes about the benefits of the activity. It gives tips on what you can do to reduce your risk of encountering mishaps while exercising.

This book also offers other tips on what else you can do to speed up the process of losing weight and maintain your ideal figure aside from Nordic walking.

Thanks again for purchasing this book. I hope you enjoy it!

Chapter 1 - Tracing the Origins of Nordic Walking

Walking using sticks was associated with infirmity and old age during the ancient times. That changed with the rise of the practice of Nordic walking – an activity that involves traversing the countryside through walking with the use of long poles that look like ski poles.

A dispute has been long-standing between the American and Finnish Nordic practitioners about the origin of Nordic walking and who invented it.

According to certain European sources, the original concept of Nordic walking was derived from how the Finnish cross-country skiers exercised using skiing poles during summer to prepare for the winter seasons in the 1930s.

Leena Jääskeläinen, a physical education lecturer from the University of Jyväskylä introduced Sauvakävely to her students in 1966. This involves walking using ski poles and it became part of the new ideas for P.E. in schools at the time. This activity was presented to the public in 1987 via the event Finlandia kävely of Finlandia Walk.

It was then that the activity captured the attention of the Finnish Central Association for Recreation Sports and Outdoor Activities. A sports equipment manufacturer, Exel, helped in creating the kind of poles needed in this new kind of walking exercise.

Another Finnish played an important role in disseminating information about the activity. A former Finnish cross-country skiing head coach, Mauri Repo, integrated the activity in his training methods for the off-season cross-country ski training in 1979. The technique that he used back then is still being used by the Nordic Walking practitioners up to now.

In 1985, the activity with the same methods as Nordic but with a different name, Exerstriding, was started in America by its inventor, Tom Rutlin. Exerstriding is exercising in a simultaneous fashion using all the muscles of the body while walking using specially designed poles.

Nowadays, you will find sources that attribute the origins of Nordic walking to the Finnish but there are also those who say that the Americans first brought it out to the public's consciousness.

In 1997, three organizations from Finland joined forces and collaborated in designing poles intended for health walking. They aimed to encourage people who were not health buffs to participate and start exercising. These three organizations that commercially reinvented and reframe the Nordic walking technique are:

- Exel, a Finnish sports equipment manufacturer that also made cross-country skiing poles. They created the prototypes of walking poles with special straps and tips and had the appropriate measurement intended to make walking comfortable. These poles were tested by athletes by doing uphill-downhill exercises like what the cross-country skiers do for summer training. The activity found out that the poles made by Exel were effective in raising the pulse rate at levels that activated different muscles in the upper body and legs, and improved the heart and circulation systems. It was Exel that launched the trademark, Walker, the lineup of walking poles made of durable but light materials.

- The Sport Institute of Finland (Vierumäki), a national training and coaching center for physical education and sports. They develop and produce advanced coaching and training services not only to Finland but all over the world. The institute was headed by the Ministry of Education and Culture.

- Finnish Central Association for Recreational Sports and Outdoor Activities (Suomen Latu). They promote outdoor activities that aim to heighten people's awareness and interest in exercise. They did not only develop techniques for outdoor exercises but they also help in maintaining and improving the quantity and quality of the hiking pathways in Finland.

It was challenging at first to distribute the poles because Finnish sports retailers did not want to sell them. Exel turned things around by creating a demand among Finnish people to look for the equipment. It began in the autumn of 1997 when Exel, as per the directives of Suomen Latu, gave around 1000 poles to educate people about the activity and raise awareness about its benefits. Walking events were held and soon enough, more people were getting interested in learning more about the walking exercise.

Through word of mouth, the Nordic walking activity reached a whole new level of popularity in the country. It led to the increased demand of the walking poles made by Exel. At first, people were afraid to go outdoors to try Nordic walking. The problem was addressed by extensive publicity using various mediums that focused on the benefits of the activity.

Exel also sponsored scientific research by the Cooper Institute in Dallas to strengthen the claims about the benefits of Nordic walking. The research found out that the activity has more benefits than ordinary walking. It gives stability to people with balance problems and orthopedic condition. The activity also got the public support of doctors, which strengthened its credibility and further raised its popularity.

By the latter part of 1998, around 4 percent of Finland's population practiced Nordic walking on a regular basis. It was hailed as the 7th most popular sports hobby among adults in Finland by 2002.

From Finland, Nordic walking was introduced to the rest of the Scandinavia as part of Exel's product expansion. Its popularity inevitably spread throughout Europe. It was at this point the Exel renamed the activity from Sauvakävely to Nordic walking. The walking poles that were named as Walker were renamed to

Nordic walker. This move played an important role for the activity to catch global attention.

The International Nordic Walking Association (INWA), which was later changed to Federation was founded in 2000 by Raija Laukkanen, Aki Karihtala, Marko Kantaneva, and Vesa-Pekka Sarparanta. The International Nordic Walking Federation has been the only non-profit international organization authorized by the founders of Nordic walking to develop, promote, and disseminate information about Nordic Walking around the globe. To date, INWA has member organizations in more than 20 countries.

Through the years, more walkers around the world became interested in the activity that caused a dramatic increase in the number of walkers and instructors. As per the statistics from INWA, the global participation in Nordic walking rose from 160,000 in 1998 to 10 million in 2012.

Most of the walkers are middle-aged and elderly individuals. They preferred the activity for its simplicity and accessibility.

How the activity is accepted depends on the culture of the country. In Japan, for example, it is not practiced in the streets but only confined to leisure resorts. In France and Germany, it is accepted as a risk-free and safe method of engaging with nature. In America, the activity is performed to get in shape and for fitness.

So what's in store for Nordic walking in the future?

It is considered a game changer as it was able to encourage various groups of populations to walk for fitness. It also changed the rural and urban scenes in many countries across the globe.

In 2003, the Nordic walker brand of poles paved the way for the Nordic Fitness Sports platform. It embraces both the winter and summer sports that enhance the upper and lower parts of the body through various exercise programs. They include the following:

- Nordic blading – the activity involves inline skating with the use of Nordic blader poles with specially designed angles.
- Nordic snowshoeing – the exercise is similar to Nordic walking because it requires the use of poles and snowshoes.

Another proof of the popularity and recognition of Nordic walking is the development of activities based on its technique. One good example is BungyPump, a modern version of walking with poles. The difference is that when the poles are pressed down. They provide extra resistance to the body with their built-in suspension system.

Chapter 2 - The Importance of Walking and Other Tips to Lose Weight

Before trying to walk using specially designed poles, you must first condition your body and start walking as a form of exercise.

Benefits of Walking

Before the advent of Nordic walking, the simple activity of walking that most people normally do every day is already recognized as a popular recreational activity and sports for people of all ages no matter where you are from. As you get older, you will have more reasons to walk more often or do it at least 30 minutes each day.

Walking can be done by people of various ages and fitness levels. You can of course challenge yourself later on by doing variations of it, including Nordic walking, but the most important thing is to get started with it.

The activity offers a lot of health benefits, which include the following:

- It makes the muscles and joints stronger.
- It improves your blood circulation and heart rate.
- It makes the bones stronger and decreases your risk of having osteoporosis.
- It is an effective weight loss technique.
- It improves your balance.
- It alleviates stress, helps clear your mind and boosts your self-esteem.
- It promotes overall health and well-being.

Walking is actually recommended not only to healthy individuals but also those who are at risk of or are already suffering from weight problems, type 2 diabetes, and cardiovascular conditions.

How do you begin establishing walking as part of your health routine?

For beginners, it is best if you will not look at it as a form of exercise. Enjoy the process and make it a social activity. Do it in groups and walk with your peers. You can also opt to join a walking group in your community.

Here are the steps on how to engage yourself in walking as part of your health routine:

1. Make it a habit. Choose the time of the day that is most convenient for you to walk.

2. Do not force yourself walk longer than you comfortably can. Take it easy. You can gradually increase the time that you dedicate on this activity as your body gets used to it.

3. Do not panic if you missed a scheduled walk. Just continue doing it when time permits.

4. Make sure that you are well protected, especially when walking outdoors. Wear the appropriate gears and always apply sunscreen on your skin.

5. Practice the proper breathing techniques as you walk. Breathe in deeply in four paces and breathe out in four paces. Practice this technique until you have developed a rhythm.

6. Stay motivated and keep track of your progress. If you are finding it hard to keep your focus when walking alone, you can tag your dog along. You can also join groups of walkers or ask friends to walk with you.

7. Do not get impatient with the results. It takes hard work to succeed and this also applies to walking. Just do it regularly and you will begin to feel its benefits after 3 to 6 weeks.

If you have any health concerns, ask your doctor first if it is okay for you to perform regular walking exercises. If you think that you are fit to do it, start with the activity at any chance that you can get.

Explore your local area. Try walking in areas you are familiar and unfamiliar with, but make sure first that these areas are safe. Walk in different pathways, such as the pavements, nature walks, parks, bush walks, and more. See the sights and appreciate nature as you engage in the activity.

Pick up your own pace. You will begin with brisk walking that offers same benefits as the other forms of an aerobic exercise. The exercise is good for the heart. It becomes more beneficial as you increase your speed and in the process, try to swing your arms, stride, breathe properly, and correct your posture.

After you have developed a routine and walking has become part of your lifestyle, it will be easier for you to try Nordic walking.

Get Moving

If you want to lose weight, you have to be serious with the top three factors that can help you in shedding off the unwanted pounds – sleep, diet, and exercise. Walking is the kind of exercise, which proves that a fancy equipment is not needed to become fit. You can begin with it while you are still learning more about Nordic walking and while you are still searching for the right poles. Remember that in order to lose weight and make your body healthier and stronger, you need to burn more calories than what you take.

You can already burn about 360 calories by walking for 45 minutes at 4 miles per hour pace. This exercise is beneficial not only for overweight individuals but also those who are suffering from heart ailments.

It is ideal for healthy adults to do moderate aerobic exercises, such as brisk walking and swimming for at least 2 hours and 30 minutes per week. You can also opt to do more vigorous exercises, such as running and cycling, for at least an hour and 15 minutes each week.

If you haven't been exercising for a while, walking can help you get back on track. This is one of the easiest forms of exercises. You can challenge yourself as you get used to the activity by walking farther and faster. Once you have the right poles, you can also begin doing Nordic walking.

Aside from walking, here are the other exercises that you can do to speed up the process of losing weight while building your strength and improving your overall health.

1. Running. It helps the bones and connective tissues to become stronger. This exercise can burn up to 600 calories per hour. You can do an interval training of performing brief spurts at certain points while you are running if you want to burn more calories.

2. Swimming. Doing this exercise vigorously for an hour can burn 400 to

700 calories. This is also effective in building and toning your muscles. This is a good exercise for women who are in the last trimester of their pregnancy and also for people who are suffering from musculoskeletal problems, arthritis, and obesity.

3. Jumping rope. An hour of this exercise can burn more than 800 calories. Aside from making your bones and joints stronger, it also works on your legs, arms, and core.

4. Kettlebell. This hardcore workout can help you burn more than 400 calories in 30 minutes. It also makes your core stronger and improves your balance and posture.

5. Cycling. This can help you burn 350 to 1000 calories in an hour, depending on your speed, terrain, and on your weight. It stimulates the release of endorphins and makes the lower part of the body stronger.

6. Push-ups. Fifty counts of this exercise can burn up to 100 calories.

Eating Right

Aside from having a regular exercise routine, whether it is solely dedicated to Nordic walking or you alternately perform it with the other activities effective in burning calories, it is essential that you team it up with proper diet. Proper diet is not about avoiding food but learning the right kinds of food that suit your age, health, and fitness goals.

One of the best kinds of diet that can help you lose weight fast is the low-carb, moderate fat, and high protein variety. For most people, the ideal amount of protein is about 1 gram per kilo of your body weight, except for those who are into strength training exercises. If you regularly perform strength training activities, you have to consume 1.7 grams of protein per kilo of your body weight.

A high-protein diet suppresses your appetite and boosts your metabolism rate by up to 100 per day. Your carb intake, on the other hand, must be limited to 20 to 50 grams each day.

Eating a high-protein meal after a 30-minute exercise can help your muscles recover at a faster rate. Here are some foods that are good sources of protein:

- Eggs. One medium egg has 6 grams of protein. You can prepare them in a variety of ways.
- Milk. This is an example of a dairy food that contains a good amount of protein and calcium.
- Pork. It contains leucine that comprises one-third of muscle protein. This speeds up muscle recovery after a strenuous activity.
- White meat. Some samples are chicken and poultry that contain high amounts of lean protein.

- Seafood and fish. Aside from being good sources of protein, they also have low amounts of fat.
- Soya. This helps in lowering your cholesterol levels and is beneficial to the heart.
- Beans and pulses. They are not only rich in protein but also in iron and fiber.

Here are the other diet tips that you must remember in order to maximize the effects of diet and your preferred exercise routine:

1. Reduce your sugar and carb intake.

Reducing your body's production of insulin will help you lose weight. This is because of the hormone, insulin, stores most of your fat. By having less insulin in your system, your body will burn fats instead of carbs. This will also prod the kidneys to get rid of excess sodium and water. As a result, you will lose the extra weight that is a result of water and bloating.

Avoid drinking fruit juices and any drinks that contain too much sugar. For dessert, you can still have a portion of your favorite treat, such as a chocolate cake. Eat slow and let the food linger on your tongue before swallowing. This will control your urge to reach out for more.

2. Add more spices to your food.

Spices are effective in curbing your hunger. For example, chilies contain capsaicin that triggers the release of endorphins in the brain. As a result, you will feel full faster while feeling good about yourself.

When you are trying to lose weight, it is best to reduce your salt intake. Salt boosts your food cravings and it makes you thirstier. Take salt in moderation.

3. Keep yourself hydrated all the time.

Water is the healthiest drink and drinking sufficient amount of fluids has a good effect on the skin. Make it a habit to drink water 30 minutes before eating a full meal. This is an effective technique that can boost your weight loss by up to 44 percent.

It is better to start Nordic walking when you already have developed the kind of mindset that is focused on your fitness goals. Any kind of exercise, which includes Nordic walking, is not always easy. If you are already a health buff – you follow the right diet and a regular exercise routine, it will be easier to try other activities that will pose more challenge and give out more health benefits in the long run.

Chapter 3 - Introducing Yourself to Nordic Walking

Walking can help you lose weight. Nordic walking can help you lose even more weight.

Nordic walking is done using a pair of long poles like how you do when you ski, but the big difference is that you don't wear the ski attire and you don't use skis. This is a method of walking wherein you use your full body. You propel yourself forward by using a pair of long poles. The price of the poles is more affordable than skis.

The activity can help you burn up to 50 percent more calories than when you do regular walking exercises. In this exercise, you can burn up to 500 calories in an hour without exerting too much force on the joints like you would do when you jog.

Aside from losing weight, Nordic walking helps athletes to prepare and condition themselves. It is also advisable for people with mobility problems.

Every push that you make with the poles gives your chest, back, shoulders, and arms a good workout. It helps in sculpting and making your upper body leaner. It also helps in working out your legs, butt, and abs. This is not only an effective way of losing weight, but it also makes your heart healthier and stronger.

Your normal heart rate is at around 5 to 17 beats per minute. When walking, it becomes 130 beats per minute and it increases by 13 percent when your do Nordic walking and becomes 147 beats per minute. You are able to consume more energy by walking with poles as compared to normal walking without poles. The activity releases muscle tension and pain, especially in the shoulder/neck area. It helps in improving the neck and spine's lateral mobility.

The muscle groups that are mostly used in Nordic walking include the rear part of the shoulders, flexor and forearm muscles, the broad back, and large pectoral muscles. It unloads weight on the knees and joints. Aside from the health benefits, the poles are safe to use even on slippery surfaces.

An Overview of How to Get Started with Nordic Walking

From being only known for a few people in one country, Nordic walking is now an outdoor activity that is enjoyed by millions of people worldwide. Here's a brief guide on how you can begin with the process.

1. Find and buy the right poles. It is important that you get poles that are specifically created for this kind of walking in order to maximize its health benefits. There are certain people who use regular

ski poles when doing Nordic walking. While this can be done, especially when you still don't have the correct poles, it puts you at a high risk of encountering problems and accidents. The Nordic walking poles have different attachments for the bottom depending on the kind of terrain you'd be walking on. They also have the proper hand straps and measured depending on your height.

Remember the following when choosing and buying your own poles:

- The poles have to fit your height, built, and stride. You have to feel comfortable when using these poles. Look into the types and try them out first. Some poles are adjustable and some are not. Try walking using the poles to see which type you'd feel most comfortable with before you buy anything. If you choose the kind that is not adjustable, have them fit perfectly to your form before leaving the store.

- Choose the poles with wrist straps that feel secure and comfortable. The straps make it easy for you to release without dropping them on your backstroke. The straps help in letting go of the poles after each push.

- The attachment at the bottom of the pole is interchangeable. Use rubber pads when walking on pavement and metal spike when walking on dirt.

In the beginning, it will be easier to perform Nordic walking on pavements. After you have gotten the hang of the exercise, you can try doing this on hiking trails and other terrains. The activity works as an alternative to walking sticks when done in the mountains. Make sure that you wear the right shoes depending on where and how far you plan to walk.

2. Use the straps to attach the poles to your wrist. These straps are important in

keeping you secured and safe no matter how challenging the terrain is. When it is your first time to walk using the poles, try to walk like usual. Hold the poles lightly but try your best to ignore them. This will help in training your body to walk normally despite the existence of the poles.

3. Begin your step on the heel. As you do so, plant the opposite arm holding the pole to the ground. This will allow the pole to push your body. Move your arms in the same rhythm as your lead foot. There has to be a unity between the lead foot and your arms. As you walk, make sure that the poles touch the ground. Lightly touch the poles to the ground as your arms move along with your lead foot while you keep your arms at a 45-degree angle. The motion will eventually feel natural. Through practice, it will be easier to propel your body forward with each push of your arms to the poles. Once you get the hang of it, you will be able to lift off the pressure

from your back and the joints in your legs by engaging your upper body.

4. Try to stand still and feel your torso with your hands while keeping your hips and head straight. Gently turn the rib cage from right to the opposite direction. Keep this rotation as you begin to walk. Practice how the torso can move gracefully with every push of the poles.

5. This walking technique uses more muscles and burns more calories than regular walking. Start slow and walk a short distance. Give your body enough time to get used to how this is being done. You can walk farther later on, but for the first few days, practice by walking at a short distance from home.

 Listen to your body to know if it is time for you to try walking at longer distances. From 30 minutes, you can begin doing the activity for an hour over a week period. Stop when your body tells you to and when you are already feeling tired and sore.

Sample of a Weekly Nordic Walking Workout Plan

1. Make it simple on your first day Choose an easy trail and avoid uphill paths. Focus on your technique and form, and walk at a pace like how you normally walk. Walk for 30 minutes.

2. Allot an hour for your second day of Nordic walking. Walk like usual and substitute the pace with long strides every 15 minutes. This technique will help in burning more calories. Continue to focus on your technique and form, and think of your your normal pace as your rest period. You don't have to finish the whole 1 hour for this day. Listen to your body and stop when you are already fatigued or something feels not right.

3. Walk for half an hour without your poles. This will reinforce your normal pace of walking. Take this time to prepare your body for more rigorous walking in the coming days.

4. Choose a rolling terrain and walk the path for an hour. Pace yourself so that you will spend the same time walking uphill and downhill.

5. You will only walk for 40 minutes on this day. Focus on the technique above anything else.

6. Rest your body and do not perform Nordic walking. Take this time to prepare for your longest walk of the week.

7. On the last day of the week, spend 75 minutes for the exercise. Push yourself to know how far you can go. Walk on trails or challenging terrains.

Through the days, you will keep adding more minutes to the exercise. Try to find challenging and difficult pathways and trails near you.

Focusing on Your Form

Nordic walking requires the coordination of your arms and legs. Here are some tips to get this done:

1. Carry and drag.

Grasp each pole that your hand is holding. Allow your arms swing gently in opposite direction as your legs when you walk with the poles alongside you. Walk slowly but do not stop until the motion feels natural. Strap on the poles. Open your hands when you walk and allow the poles drag from behind.

2. Plant and push.

Plant the poles firmly to the surface. Hold the grips lightly as you keep the 45-degree angle of the poles behind you. Keep your elbows near your body and your arms in a straight position. Try to relax your body, especially your arms. Keep your attention on the pole's contact to the ground. As the walking becomes more natural, push the poles behind in every step. The force will come through the strap and each push has to be firm. As you push your arm beneath your hip by the end of an arm swing, make sure that you open up your hand. Reach out your arm to the front when it's time to swing the arm forward as if you are trying to hold someone else's hand.

3. Practice and perfect your form.

The person standing at your back must see the sole of your shoe each time that you push off. Slightly lean to the front using your ankles for support and try to make each stride longer. This way, you will achieve a better leg workout with a fuller arm swing.

Nordic Walking Tips

Are you ready to try Nordic walking? Remember the following tips when you have taken the plunge:

- Try to walk as naturally as you can.
- Relax your shoulders as you move.
- Do not hold the grip too tight.
- Keep the poles and your hands close to your body.
- Always keep the poles in a diagonal position.
- The movement of the right foot and left arm and the left foot and right arm must always be in unison.
- Push the pole behind in line with your pelvis.
- At the end of each push to the pole, make sure that you open the palm of your hands.
- After each push, you have to quickly bring the pole forward again.

- Unroll your feet from the heel to your toes.

Always remember to perform warm-up exercises before doing Nordic walking. Each session is long and takes about 60 to 90 minutes. Develop a steady pace. Perform cool down exercises after each session to give your body time to relax before going back to your usual daily routine.

Mastering the Important Techniques in Nordic Walking

Arm swing

This is one of the foundations of this activity's technique. It looks easy to do but many beginners find it hard to perfect. A good arm swing is relaxed but powerful. The movement has to begin from the shoulder. This is same as for normal walking but in this case, the arm swing is a progressive action and is more prominent.

First, practice your forward arm movement. When you are Nordic walking, most of the power will come from the arms when the pole is in front of your body.

Next, you have to give more effort to your back swing. When you push the pole behind your hips, its tip must be in a straight line with your shoulder. To get this done, you have to gather force from your upper arm. This may be hard at first but you can attain this form through continued practice.

What are the benefits of a good arm swing?

- It makes the shoulder and your upper arm muscles stronger. The shoulder joint can perform the greatest range of motion among all the joints in the body but this is also the most complicated. This is the part that is also commonly injured when you did not do the activity properly. Nordic walking works on the muscles found between your shoulder blades. It makes the shoulder muscles stronger, stabilizes your shoulders, and in effect, improves your posture.

- It improves the body's circulatory function. The activity boosts the supply of oxygenated blood to the tissues and muscles. It is also responsible for the proficient return of the blood through the veins and into your heart. In order to get the most benefits for your circulatory function, you have to perform the proper arm swing, learn how to squeeze and release the hand around the pole handle, and perform the heel/toe roll properly.

- When you perform proper arm swing in Nordic walking, you engage your diaphragm to breathe properly. In effect, it drains the lymph. This is beneficial for everybody, especially those who are suffering from with lymphedema. The body's lymphatic system is important to the immune system and gives you protection against diseases and infection. There are clusters of lymph nodes in the body, which include the area beneath the armpits that benefit the most from doing the proper arm swing.

- As you perfect the arm swing when you do Nordic walking, you will get faster and be able to perform more rotation. This is a good workout to improve core strength and in making your abs flat and toned.

Here are the top factors to remember in order to improve your arm swing:

1. Do not overdo it. The movement has to feel natural. Avoid the common mistakes of clamping the shoulder too tightly to the side of your body. Swing from the shoulder

and not from your elbow. Let the movement come freely.

2. When you swing your arm, do it like how you would when doing a low handshake with the person in front of you. Do not over-reach because this can cause the misalignment of your shoulder.

3. Perfect the hand squeeze action by practicing your hand control. In the beginning, you can do single arm poling to practice the technique.

4. As you go along the exercise, you have to make your arm swing faster in order to push the pole behind you. This works in toning your shoulders and is also a good workout for your triceps. Practice rotating your torso as you swing an arm in order to get a good frame swing.

5. Make it a habit to stretch your chest muscles as you walk. This is good for your posture and will reduce the risk of injuring your pectoral muscles.

Chest Workout

It is important to exercise the chest in order to avoid slumping or slouching. Your goal is to lift the chest to the right position by stretching out its tight muscles. This workout gives out the following benefits:

- It improves your posture. When your chest is often slumped, the tendency of the body is to get misaligned. This body posture causes a lot of back problems.
- The workout strengthens your core. This is effective in trimming your

waist by twisting. It happens as the space around your waist gets bigger as you lift your chest.

- When you walk with an open chest, you will have an easier time doing the proper breathing technique. You will specifically notice the improvement when you are walking uphill. Poor breathing results to stress and cellular inefficiency. They happen because the amount of oxygen in the cellular level is insufficient.
- Your speed will improve after perfecting the workout.

How do you work out the chest?

1. Make the spine longer. Elongate the length of your spine as if you are trying to separate the vertebrae and discs.

2. Keep the distance between your shoulders.

3. Keep the gap between the bottom of your rib cage and hip bones as long as you can, especially when walking in an uphill direction.

4. Bring your chest to the front as you walk.

Focusing on Your Hips and Pelvis

To make your hip/pelvis area more stable, you have to develop a good workout routine for your hip flexors and glutes. This is necessary for the safety of your back and lower body and for long-term mobility. Spending too much time sitting down leads to the tightness of the hip flexors. As a result, your glutes cannot function properly and become weaker. This does not only make the pelvis and hips unstable, it causes pains in the knees, hips, and groin.

Here are the proper steps to exercise the hip/pelvis area of the body:

1. Stand firmly and tall while keeping the gap between the bottom of the rib cage and top of the hip bone long.

2. Pull your navel to the direction of your spine while keeping the level of your hips. Do not put down your chest.

3. Keep on rolling through your foot. Feel the stretch across to upper area of the foot while keeping an ankle open as you push off using your toes.

4. As you push off with your toes, squeeze your glutes and push into the hips. You will know that you are doing the exercise right once you feel the stretch in your hip flexor or at the top of your thigh.

Wrists

The load that you bear in Nordic walking is a good exercise for the bones and wrists. Keep in mind that wrists are delicate. Since you only move them forward and backward during the activity, you also have to load them in other directions. It will also help to make wrist stretches part of your daily exercise regime.

How to get this done:

1. As you push, make sure that your wrist is straight and firm. Do not flex it and hold the firmness as the pressure travels through it.

2. Check you can use the strap to make it more beneficial to your wrist. You can power through the position of the strap near the forefinger and thumb, which is close to the handle of the pole. This gives less stress to your wrist joint. You can also try to power through the bottom of your hand.

3. Practice how to squeeze and release the pole handle when you close and open your hand. The movement is similar to how you squeeze a stress ball. This strengthens your fingers and wrists.

4. Improve the flexibility of your wrists by performing stretches that lengthen and strengthen your arm including your wrists.

It can't be helped that there are times when your wrists feel sore. During these times, push gently through the strap and avoid stressing your wrists any further.

Chapter 4 - The Needed Gears and Equipment in Nordic Walking

After learning the proper techniques of Nordic walking, make sure that you have the right gear to get started with it.

Choosing the Right Nordic Walking Poles

The long poles offer stability, which improves safety while walking. This is recommended to people with different workout levels, even those who are only beginning to get serious about in keeping fit. The routine is considered low-impact and easy-to-follow so long as you have the right guide on what to do.

There are specifically designed poles for Nordic walking so make sure that you don't use skis intended for slopes. These long poles come in two types, adjustable and non-adjustable. The adjustable type fits more than one user and it can easily be stored. The non-adjustable are more fit, it won't collapse all of a sudden while you are on it and this version is lighter.

So how do you choose the right poles?

These poles can be bought at specialty stores and at certain online shops. When buying online, make sure that you check the chart and choose the size of the pole that is suitable for your height. For beginners and people who are between sizes, it is recommended to settle for the shorter model because it will allow them to move easily.

Find the grip of the pole and hold it with its tip facing the ground and the pole is in a vertical position. Keep your arm close to your chest and your elbow bent at 90 degrees.

Poles have right and left models. Use the correct side, slide your hand on the strap and hold its grip. Secure the poles by wrapping any added security features, such as a Velcro strap that you need to tie around your wrist. Practice the grip. It has to be secure but not too tight.

There are other features of the poles that you must learn to use properly. These poles have rubber tips that are intended for paved surfaces. Remove these rubber tips when walking in snow, dirt, grass or sand, to achieve better traction.

Choosing the Right Length for Poles

Here are the pole lengths and the height of the user in centimeters (feet/inches)

105 – 152.40 (5'00")

105 – 154.94 (5'01")

105 – 157.48 (5'02")

110 – 160.02 (5'03")

110 – 162.56 (5'04")

115 – 167.64 (5'06")

115 – 170.18 (5'07")

115 – 172.72 (5'08")

120 – 175.26 (5'09")

120 – 177.80 (5'10")

125 – 180.34 (5'11")

125 – 182.88 (6'00")

125 – 185.42 (6'01")

130 – 187.96 (6'02")

130 – 190.50 (6'03")

130 – 193.04 (6'04")

135 – 195.58 (6'05")

Having the right equipment allows you to maximize the benefits of the process and helps in avoiding injuries. Take note of the following when choosing Nordic walking poles:

- Choose light composite shafts that are durable.
- The angles spike tip of the poles must be correct and interchangeable.

- Choose poles with a specifically designed strap that offers support and outstanding transfer.
- Use poles with ergonomically designed grips that are capable of withstanding different surfaces.

There is a formula that is used to choose the right pole length that suits an individual for Nordic walking. The formula is your height times 0.68 and round it to the nearest lower 5 cm. When you hold the pole by the grip and with the tip on the ground, your elbow must be placed at a maximum of 90 degrees angle.

The other factors that play an important role in choosing poles include long term fitness goals, walking speed, skills, joint mobility, terrain, level of fitness, length of stride, and the proportions of your limbs.

The rubber tips that come along with these poles are best used on paved surfaces. Remove the rubber for better traction when walking in sand, grass, snow, or dirt.

Aside from Exel, many other companies are now catering to the demand for these poles. Here are some features that you have to look into when shopping for Nordic walking poles:

- The best poles are not necessarily expensive. You can get a lightweight but durable type at around $80 to $85.
- A lightweight material is ideal for longer walks. Make sure that it is strong and made of a durable carbon composite.
- The mesh strap must feel comfortable on the skin. It has to feel soft without getting your skin clammy.
- Avoid getting poles with mesh strap that is angled because you can trip when they get twisted. The mesh strap has to be slightly rounded for comfort and security.

- If you are buying adjustable poles, choose the type that can adjust from 39 to 51 or anything with that range.
- The releasable trigger straps are also great features because they make it easier for you to slip out of the poles without so much of a hassle.

How would you know that you are getting the most from your poles?

Nordic walking is a good exercise and it also gives you a perfect excuse to socialize. It can be fun, especially when done in groups. Amidst the fun, make sure that you don't forget how to get the most out of the experience, especially in using your poles. Aside from the fun, you have to keep your motivation to try harder each day.

Here are some of the ways to check if you are using your poles properly:

1. Walk at an optimum pace. Keep your focus on a specific object. It can be a tree, bench, or a lamppost in the near distance.

As you pass the object while Nordic walking, lift your poles while your legs keep on moving at the same pace. Your speed will decrease and your legs will feel heavy if you have been using the poles properly.

2. If you only observe a slight change in your speed and how your legs weigh during the test, ask your instructor to devise how you use your upper body in the activity. He/she can check what muscles you are engaging as you walk and where do you get most of your strength from. He/she can then devise the proper movements to help you utilize the power through the poles.

Walking Pole Maintenance

Here are the important steps to make sure that your poles are in good working condition all the time:

1. Occasionally wash the straps, ideally at around 40 degrees, using your washing machine.

2. Pick out any debris, grass, or wool that may have been caught by the Velcro. It is bound to lose its sticky feature, which will make it easier to come undone when you push on the strap as you walk. You can either mend them if you know how to sew or if not, it is best to replace the straps with brand new ones. Ask the store where you buy your poles if the warranty covers the replacement of the straps and for how long.

3. Keep the tips and paws of the poles free from grime and mud by washing them after every use. The build-up of these elements can affect the performance of your poles.

There are certain poles with tips that are susceptible to wear and tear. You can deal with this problem by putting an insulation tape around the shaft of the pole. You can also opt to remove them when you are planning to walk on a smooth surface. Another trick that you can do to solve the problem is to squeeze the paw at the hinge.

This will tighten its fitting against the pole. Your last option is to replace them.

The Right Footwear

When it comes to the footwear, you can choose whatever you feel comfortable with. It is important that the footwear is light and has flexible soles. Here are some of the features that many Nordic walking tutors prefer when it comes to the shoes that they wear:

- If you have narrow feet, find trial running shoes that offer superb flexibility through your forefoot, have a good grip, and decent tread.

- There are shoes with a tongue pocket that is specifically made for Nordic walking. You will tuck the shoelaces in the pocket so that the poles won't catch the lace loops when you are walking.

- Some practitioners prefer shoes with minimal features and something that will still allow them to feel the floor when worn. It makes them feel like they are going through a free foot reflexology session when they walk in these shoes. Aside from feeling the bumps and lumps of the trail, the footwear also provides a better grip when used on muddy surfaces.

These minimalist shoes provide ample balance and are effective in keeping the back in alignment. They reduce the chances of having the lower back pains during and after the activity. The best thing about these shoes is that they allow your feet to breathe and move.

- There are some Nordic walking trainers who prefer using waterproof shoes that make it easier to walk on muddy fields and wet grass. For this type of shoes, always choose the kind that is light and breathable. They are typically used during the winter season and when you are going on wet terrains.

- Older individuals feel more secure in walking using trail shoes. They give firm footing in any kinds of surfaces.

Waterproof shoes are a bit expensive over the other kinds of footwear used in Nordic walking. If the surface is wet or muddy and you can't afford these shoes, you can opt to use waterproof socks to protect your feet from getting soaked and keep them dry and warm throughout the exercise.

The Right Clothing

Your clothing for this exercise will depend on the weather. When the weather is cold and damp, your goal is to stay warm and dry. Here are the items of clothing that you have to shop for:

1. Base layer. The moisture from the next layer will seep through it and make it easier to evaporate. Always choose the type of clothing that is breathable for each layer. This way, you will not get chilled and you will feel comfortable as you go about your Nordic walking routine.

The base layer must contain anti-bacterial features so that you won't smell foul throughout the activity. The best choices of fabric for this layer include bamboo, merino wool, polyesters, and microfiber. You can buy the long-sleeved styles but it is better to invest on a short-sleeved base layer that you can use in any weather.

2. Middle layer. This layer gives your body its needed insulation. Choose anything that is not that bulky but is effective in giving warmth, such as a gilet or fleece. The material has to be lightweight and breathable. There are certain brands that offer mid layer with zips and wind proofing to make it easier for you to vent the garment when necessary.

Choose the kind that you can easily squash down and pack. This layer tends to get removed when you are already feeling warm.

3. Top layer or shell. This is the most important layer because it protects you from rain and the wind while allowing your body to breathe. This topmost part has to be windproof and waterproof. Choose the kind that you can easily stash and pack when not needed.

You can use a soft shell, which is good for everyday wear. It is generally windproof and water resistant, but won't keep you completely dry when the weather is foul. It is breathable, lightweight, and easy on the skin. It gives ample protection when there are only light rains and during chilly days.

A hard shell is advised to be worn on extremely wet days. For this type, look for the kinds that are 100 percent waterproof, with sealed zips, and, completely breathable. Fit it to your body when buying the material. Choose the size that will allow you to move freely even after wearing the other layers underneath this one.

Aside from the top layer, make it a habit to carry a pair of 100 percent waterproof overpants to keep your legs dry when the weather is bad. Choose the type with an adjustable waistband for easy fitting. You can also choose something with studs at the sides of the legs, which are easier to open and remove.

If you aren't wearing waterproof shoes, you can keep the water or snow from getting into your feet by clipping a pair of waterproof gaiters under your footwear.

To keep your head warm, you can wear a waterproof softshell hat or a thermal fleece. For the gloves, make sure that they are waterproof, flexible, and thin.

What to wear during summer or spring

The idea here is to keep yourself as comfortable as you can get. Here are some tips on how to get this done:

1. For the top half, wear layers of clothing with breathable fabrics. They keep your sweat away from your body. Do not wear cotton for the base layer. Cotton will leave you wet and feeling cold. Use shirts made from natural or synthetic fibers, such as bamboo or merino wool. During extra hot days, it is best to wear short sleeve shirts. Avoid wearing gilet not unless you have

somewhere to store it when you are already feeling hot.

2. You can use soft shell jackets with a good degree of water resistance. They will protect you from sudden rains and you can also use them as wind breakers. Choose a soft and breathable material that you can easily tie around your waist when you are feeling hot.

3. For your legs, you can opt to wear shorts or leggings but check the trails for any signs of ticks. A pair of lightweight walking trousers will keep you protected from insects or ticks that you may encounter along the way.

There are certain accessories that are essential to carry when the weather is warm. Bring a small backpack where you can put your water bottle. You can also store the discarded layers of clothing in the bag.

Wear a cap to protect your head from the sun. Do not forget to apply sunscreen with sufficient SPF before going for a walk under the heat of the sun. You can also opt to wear sunglasses.

Chapter 5 - Warm Up and Cool Down Exercises Before and After Nordic Walking

The warm up and cool down exercises in Nordic walking must focus on the muscles of the lower body, such as the hip flexor, calf, gluts, hamstring, and quadriceps. Side bends and upper back stretches are also needed to pay attention to the upper portion of the body, which includes the arm, shoulder, and chest. These exercises will speed up the body's recovery process before and after the training. They help in improving your performance, whether you are an athlete or someone who is only after leisure or personal fitness.

Warm Up

Warm up exercises are necessary to get rid of any stiffness of the muscles before you do Nordic walking. The routine is typically composed of the following:

- Increasing the body's temperature by jogging for 5 to 10 minutes.
- Reduce muscle stiffness by doing dynamic stretching movements for 10 to 15 minutes.
- For pros, prepare for the competition by following event specific drills for 10 to 15 minutes.

They help you prepare psychologically and physiologically for the exercise. When done right, they can help in preventing muscle and joint injuries. By performing these exercises, the muscles loosen up due to the increased blood flow in the cells. It boosts the force of muscular contractions and your speed. The muscles become more pliable and less stiff because the nerve impulses travel faster when you have a higher body temperature.

These exercises gradually boost your heart rate to meet the demands of your metabolic and circulatory systems once you begin walking. The initial warm up exercises are intended to improve your coordination and neural function. Make sure that the movements will only make you perspire but not fatigued. Each session usually lasts for 5 to 10 minutes and the intensity depends on your age and fitness level. The main goal of the exercises is to prepare your body and mind to meet the energetic demands of your next fitness routine.

These warm up exercises provide the following benefits:

- Reduce the stiffness of the muscles.
- Warmed muscles have a lower viscous resistance that allows greater economy of movement.
- Facilitated muscle metabolism and nerve transmission when the temperature is higher.
- Higher muscle temperature allows hemoglobin to readily release oxygen.
- Improves your focus.
- Boosts the process of relaxation and contraction of the muscles.

What are the best warm up exercises before Nordic walking?

You can begin with these simple movements that focus on the lower part of the body and arm muscles:

1. Leg swing. Stand on any leg. You can choose to begin on your left or right leg depending on your preference. Loosely swing the other leg from the hip to the front and then backward again. Relax your legs as you swing and do not bring the foot too high. You can swing each leg up to 20 times.

2. Ankle circles. Place your foot firmly on the ground and lift the other one. Flex your ankle in a slow manner by moving the ankle joint but not the lower part of the leg. Draw big circles using your toes. Do this 8 times in each direction. Switch the position of your feet and repeat the sequence.

3. Hula hoop jumps. Jump in place on both feet. Keep your shoulders and head to the front as you twist your lower body and feet to the right and then to the left. You will then go back and forth as you repeat the jumps. Jump up to 20 times while you are facing front but make sure to twist

your legs and hips to the right and left on alternate jumps.

4. Pelvic loops. Place your hands firmly on your hips. Keep your feet shoulder width apart and your body upright, as you slightly bend your knees. Make 10 slow circles using your hips. Push your hips gently to the front, left, to the back and right. Reverse the motion and repeat the sequence.

5. Arm circles. Straighten your arms to each side. Move your arms in a backward manner and make small circles during the first three counts and make the circles bigger until you have done 12. Shake your arms and go back to your original position. Repeat the sequence but move your arms forward this time.

6. Stand as high as you can on your toes. Pull up the inside parts of the feet as you roll towards the outer parts. Reverse the position of the feet and stand on your heels. Place your feet firmly on the floor.

This warm up exercise helps in reducing the risk of injuring your shin while walking.

Cool Down

The cooling down phase must be done in a gradual manner. After Nordic walking for a long period, you will need to catch your breath and bring your heart rate back to its state during the resting period. After 3 to 5 minutes, you can start stretching the muscles groups that you have utilized in your fitness routine. The cool down stretching exercises aim to delay the onset of muscle soreness and aids your body during the recovery period. Breathe deeply as you exercise to bring in more oxygen into your system.

The routine is typically composed of the following:

- Get rid of the waste products from the working muscles and decrease the temperature of your body by slowly jogging or walking for 5 to 10 minutes.
- Perform static stretching exercises for 5 to 10 minutes.

The cool down exercises lower down your blood lactic acid levels. They gradually bring your heart rate to normal and help prevent blood pooling. They help in bringing enough supply of oxygen and blood to the brain, which prevents you from fainting despite the strenuous activities that you have done.

The aim of the exercises is to bring your body back to a state of rest. It works by reducing the intensity of your physical activities.

Before stretching, walk easily or jog in place for a couple of minutes. Perform the stretches up to a point of mild discomfort but not painful. Hold each pose for 30 seconds. Keep your chest lifted and your head and shoulders to the front while you do the following:

1. Hamstring stretch. This will cool down the back of your thigh. Position your hips at the edge of a chair. Stretch a leg with your toes pointed upwards. Slowly push your chest to the front as you bend your hips. Keep your chest to the front while you hold the pose for 30 seconds. This will stretch your calf and the back of your knee and thigh without feeling any pain.

2. Calf stretch. Place your hands at the back of a chair. Put your foot in a lunge position by placing it behind you. Keep the toes of both feet straight to the front. Gently push on the heel of the back foot.

As you do, let your hips fall lightly to the front. Keep your back foot firm to the floor as you hold the pose for 30 seconds.

3. Quadriceps Stretch. Position yourself at the back of a chair. Grasp your ankle behind you while your knee is pointed down and you are standing in an upright pose. Hold this for 30 seconds.

If you are finding it hard to perform the stretching while standing, you can opt to sit with your hips placed at the edge of a chair. Turn your knees to a side while the outside part of the hip is off the chair. Place your hands at the back of the chair. Put your outside knee down to the floor with your thigh pointed down. Keep your torso straight as you slowly bring your hip to the front. Hold the pose for 30 seconds. Gently bring the knees together before repeating the sequence on the other side.

4. Side stretch. Straighten one arm with the palm pushing to the direction of the

ceiling. Gently stretch your shoulder blade and rib cage. Hold the pose for 30 seconds.

5. Backscratch. Position a hand at the back of your head. Keep the elbow pointed to the direction of the ceiling. Gently reach the other hand behind you. Move it up and back near the shoulder blades. Hold the pose for 30 seconds. Interchange your hands and repeat the sequence.

6. Chest stretch. Put your hands on your back and clasp them. Slowly push back your shoulders and you squeeze the shoulder blades. Hold the pose for 30 seconds.

Chapter 6 - The Benefits of Nordic Walking

Through the years, the rates of death due to noncommunicable diseases or NCDs continue to rise. Every year, around 15 million people around the world between the ages of 30 to 70 die prematurely due to NCDs, such as stroke, heart disease, cancer, chronic lung disease, and diabetes. Many NCDs are also lifestyle diseases – the kind brought by a sedentary lifestyle and poor diet.

This is among the reasons why everyone is encouraged to exercise and develop a healthy lifestyle. Walking is the most popular form of exercise around the globe. It is an effective health routine that lowers one's risk of suffering from NCDs.

Nordic walking poses more challenge than a regular walk and it also offers more benefits. It is most beneficial when done regularly. The activity simultaneously combines the exercise training of the upper and lower parts of the body. You will apply force to the poles through your arms in each stride. This, in effect, develops the endurance of the muscles in the shoulders, core, arms, chest, and upper back. As you increase the length of your stride and walking speed, you also boost your body's oxygen consumption.

A person's oxygen uptake or VO2 increases by up to 49 percent when Nordic walking as compared to regular walking without poles. This is due to the varying levels that you can do when walking with poles. The activity also increases your heart rate and blood pressure at healthy levels.

There are many studies which proved that the activity is beneficial for all, especially for the elderly population. Aside from helping you lose weight and in making your body stronger, it also deals with muscle weakness and lower body joint pains in an effective manner. This low-impact exercise is beneficial for wellness, health, and fitness of everyone no matter what your fitness level is.

Here are some of the proven health benefits of Nordic walking:

- It boosts your cardiovascular health.
- It utilizes 90 percent of your body muscles. You only use about 40 percent in regular walking.
- The support that you get from the poles reduces stress on your knees and hips.
- Your calorie expenditure goes higher by up to 46 percent.
- It improves the mobility of your upper body.
- It improves your balance and posture.
- It is effective in reducing pains in the shoulder, neck, and upper back.

Back Pain Rehabilitation

Continued studies and research proved that Nordic walking is effective in the rehabilitation of chronic pain in the back. It works as long as the process is supervised by a health professional who understands the underlying condition. To get the most out of it, find a Nordic walking trainer who is also a physiotherapist. They can devise a training program that is effective and safe for the patient. Regular training will lead to improved fitness and stamina. It also lowers your risk of persistent or recurrent back pain and other health problems due to an inactive lifestyle.

Nordic Walking Improves Your Mental Health

The exercise helps in improving your focus and other mental processes, such as remembering, thinking, and understanding. The activity affects a person's mental health through the following:

- It increases a person's energy levels.
- It effectively reduces physical symptoms of anxiety.
- It helps in improving the quality of your sleep.
- It gives you better cognitive performance at school.
- It improves your affective response that results to increased psychological wellness that helps people suffering from type 2 diabetes.
- It slows down the cognitive decline of elderly individuals and improves their cognitive performance.
- The exercise is generally good for the memory because in increases the size of a person's hippocampus and prefrontal cortex.

Recommended for People with Type 2 Diabetes

Make sure that you are guided by a trainer who will devise a program that suits your health if you have this kind of chronic condition. Nordic walking helps people with Types 2 diabetes by:

- Controls the fasting and post-walk levels of your blood sugar.
- Boosts your fitness levels and make your heart and respiratory system healthier.

Studies proved that inactivity worsens the condition. If you aren't up for the challenge of Nordic walking, you can begin by simply doing regular walks on a regular basis. Once you have developed the habit of exercising for health, it will be easier to adapt other forms of healthy activities.

Improves Your Cardiovascular Health

Regular walking offers many benefits to your cardiovascular health. Nordic walking doubles the benefits because it requires you to use all the muscle groups in your body. It affects your cardiovascular health by:

- It decreases your body weight – waist circumference, BMI, and body fat percentage.
- It increases your good cholesterol (HDL) and lowers the bad (LDL).
- It boosts the endurance of your muscles.
- It lowers your risk of suffering from coronary heart disease.
- It lowers your blood pressure.
- It increases your body's aerobic capacity.

How Nordic Walking Prevents and Lowers Your Chances of Having Other NCDs

Certain studies proved that this kind of vigorous physical activity, especially when done regularly, helps in preventing cancer, such as colon and breast cancer. This is also recommended for people who have survived cancer in order to keep their health in top shape.

For cancer survivors, it is important to remember that you have to gradually get back to being active rather than spend too much time resting after your ordeal. Listen to your body when it can already perform the needed movements for Nordic walking. If not, you can settle for less tiring activities to prepare your body for more challenging tasks in the coming days.

Aside from cancer, the activity is also effective in dealing with other NCDs, which include the following:

- It reduces the pain of your arthritis.
- It lowers your chances of getting admitted due to chronic lung disease.
- It improves your mobility, which is beneficial to your overall health.

Nordic Walking with the Pros

Aside from getting the right gears, it is important that you learn the techniques of Nordic walking from a qualified trainer. This is the best way to maximize the benefits that you get from doing the activity. You can always go alone or form groups to walk with, but it is not advisable in the beginning.

A trainer will advise you about the proper use of the poles. He/she can devise training plans depending on your health, age, and fitness levels. These trainers will show you how to properly place the poles for propulsion. They will adjust the techniques according to your progression and the kind of pathways or terrains that you are walking into. They will teach you the basics about the activity, look out for your safety, and monitor your improvement.

The teaching methods vary depending on the kind of class that you enroll in and where you are. At first, you'd be placed along with other beginners in a small class environment. This way, you won't feel pressured of keeping up all the time, which is likely to happen if you will be grouped with the more experienced walkers.

The classes are typically grouped according to every individual's ability and fitness goals. Doing this along with a class will motivate you to show up at each session and will encourage you to improve. Through time, your trainer will increase the activity of your training by incorporating the following:

- Increase your walking speed.
- Require more arm movements and propulsion.
- Increase the time and covered distance.
- Trying out the more challenging terrains and environments.
- Adding more exercises with the walking circuits.

Functional and Physiological Effects of the Exercise

Nordic walking adds intensity to regular walking or using the treadmill to exercise. It results in the increased oxygen consumption and caloric expenditure. Despite the added challenge of using the poles, it is said that the state of overexertion in doing this exercise is difficult to reach.

For elderly patients, the trainers adjust the poles so that they can be brought forward, a position which offers more stability and balance for the walkers. The placement of the poles is less inclined but the arms and legs still move in an alternate fashion.

The Nordic walking training program can also be integrated into a cardiac rehabilitation exercise training program. This aims to provide a program that suits the needs and health requirements of each patient.

The use of the poles in walking adds variety, interest, and challenge in the program along with the following factors:

1. Safety. The activity is generally safe for as long as it is done with proper supervision and you are using the right equipment and gears.

2. It utilizes different measures to evaluate your progress. If you are doing this due to a health problem, you will be given a questionnaire to determine how you are coping with it and if you are getting better or not. For example, patients with chronic obstructive pulmonary disease and chronic neck pain are given SF 36

questionnaire to measure the quality of life. The advancement of the COPD group is measured via the Hospital Anxiety and Depression scale. Fibromyalgia patients, on the other hand, are given the Fibromyalgia Impact questionnaire to compare their fitness levels before and after, as well as to monitor their improvement.

For the elderly and most walkers with other forms of chronic diseases, they are given the 6-minute walk test to evaluate their progress.

3. Addressing the demands of related jobs. This is an activity that is most beneficial to people whose jobs require them to walk a lot. Nordic walking is used as part of the conditioning process to help these people to meet the physical demand of their jobs. The fitness training boosts their confidence and supports them throughout their fitness training. Some samples of the jobs that have significant walking demands include rescue service, nursing,

countryside rangers, postman, bin men, builders, and street cleaner.

4. The activity is integrated as part of a patient's physical therapy. This can be a part or an addition to rehabilitation and normal physiotherapy. It reinforces the aspects of the therapy without any negative effect. This is typically used as a form of rehabilitation of movement problems. If this is the case, find a Nordic walking instructor who is also a physiotherapist. This way, your trainer can devise goal oriented programs that can increase your general physical activity and confidence.

As the training progresses, your program will be adjusted to increase its intensity via technique, speed, terrain, distance, circuits, exercises, and intervals. It pushes you to become better without putting your safety at risk.

Chapter 7 – Learning More about the Right Techniques of Nordic Walking

There are many techniques that you need to learn in order maximize the benefits of the activity. It may look simple – you will go from point A to point B. The question is how will you do that efficiently and without injuring yourself?

To begin with, make sure that you remember and apply the following pointers:

1. Every time your foot lands on the ground, make sure that the heel strikes first. The center of the heel must land to the ground first before the other parts of the foot. Practice this technique by paying attention to how each foot lands when you walk.

2. The ball of the foot refers to the base of your toes. When your foot rolls onto it, your heel will automatically come off the ground.

Practice the first two steps with one foot at a time. Perfect the proper way of landing a foot and the correct way of lifting it off.

3. Rock and roll. When your heel touches the ground, the rest of your foot must continue rolling. Try to stand still with both feet firm on the ground. Imagine that you are a rocking chair and rock your feet from the heel to the toes in a back and

forth manner. When you are Nordic walking, it is easy to determine the sounds of the feet that are not rolling because when they do, your feet will barely make any sounds. When you hear slapping sounds, it means that you are doing it wrong. You have to improve the technique to prevent your shins from getting sore.

4. To propel your body forward, you have to push the ball of your foot down and back again to the ground. While the foot is pushed, one side of your buttocks should feel tight.

5. As you walk, your body has to lean to the front as a single unit as if you are completely falling forward. Put your weight at the balls of your feet. Do not round your body at the back and avoid bending from the waist. You will notice that your speed will increase once you have mastered this technique.

6. Begin the activity by walking leisurely. After a while, you have to focus on the

movements of your legs and arms. Always make sure that each sway of the arm must meet the opposite leg. This technique is not really new because it is the natural walking rhythm that many people fail to observe.

7. The arm swing has to be straight and even. Focus on this technique after you have perfected the rhythm of the leg and arm when walking. Swing your arm in an even manner in both directions. You can ask someone to observe if you are doing this properly. You can also practice at home in front of a mirror to check if you are swinging your arms back and forth evenly.

8. As you walk, perform a slight rotation at your rib cage without stopping what you are doing. Practice the movement first by standing with both feet on the ground. Put your hands below your chest and feel your rib cage. Keep your hips forward and your head to the front. Gently turn the rib cage from right to left. As you twist, feel your

solar plexus where the action is taking place. Keep on doing the twisting movement as you release your hands.

Go back to walking at your normal pace. When you are ready, slightly rotate your rib cage without stopping or slowing down. Your right arm will naturally move forward as you slightly rotate your torso to the left and vice versa.

9. Always maintain your balance while walking. Keep your body stable, especially when you are rotating your torso. Make sure that your shoulder blades are stable and your core is activated in the duration of the walk.

10. Do not go beyond your speed. Your speed will eventually increase through continued practice and application of the right techniques. The average walking pace in Nordic walking is at around 5 km/hour. This is relatively slower than the speed in brisk walking, which is 6.5 km/hour.

You are being evaluated based on your speed but you have to let it come naturally. Do not walk any faster when you feel like your body is not up to it. This will only give you stress and might cause certain mishaps that could have been avoided. The idea here is do not over stride, which is a common mistake for many walkers. The action will not feel right and you won't be able to concentrate on the other things that you ought to do with the movement of your feet, arm, and torso.

Instead of focusing too much on your speed, always pay attention that your foot is actively rolling from the heel to the toe. Push your body firmly with the strength coming from your toes. Quickly push back using your pole while making sure that you are pushing down to the ground. Gather strength from the muscles of your middle back and triceps. Continue with the process each time to do Nordic walking and your speed will naturally increase over time.

11. Focus on yourself and do not compare your abilities to others. You have to move according to the pace that your body feels comfortable with. This way, you can utilize the movements and your breathing at the same time.

You will know that you are walking at the right pace when you are still comfortable in talking short sentences while doing the exercise. It is okay to catch your breath after a few sentences but it is a different thing when you can no longer talk at all while walking because you are always gasping for breath.

Basic Troubleshooting Guide

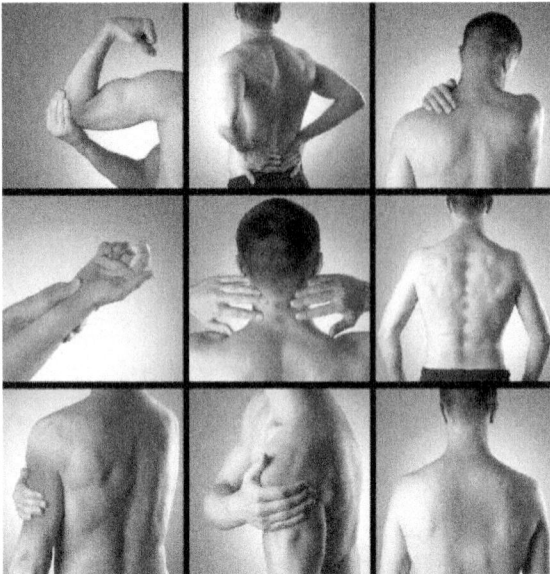

Even the seasoned Nordic walkers experience certain issues with the activity. Here are some of the most commonly encountered problems and how to deal with them:

1. Painful forearms

It is a common mistake in the beginning to use the strap the wrong way and grip the poles with too much force. These actions will hurt your forearms, which you will only be aware of once you are done walking. Always remember not to use your hand when pushing and propelling your body forward but the force should be applied to the strap. Your hand is naturally gripping the handle of the pole as you plant it in the ground. Once done, relax the hand and use the force of the heel of the hand to the strap.

2. Stiff shoulders and neck

This is a usual problem in the beginning. You are putting too much attention on the rules and other technicalities of the action. This results in your neck and shoulder muscles getting stiff. Nordic walking, in the long run, will ease away the tension and pain. While you are only starting out, keep in mind the following tips:

- Keep the gap between your shoulders and earlobes as far as you can but make sure that you are comfortable and pain-free. Lift your head off the shoulders at the same time that you drop your shoulders.

- Your head must be placed in the middle with your ears parallel to your shoulders and never ahead of them. Avoid sticking your neck out. It will strain the muscles in the neck that will cause the pain.
- Feel the tension in your neck and shoulders as it drains down to the direction of your tummy. This will leave you with a light feeling as if you are responsible in easing the tension away.

3. Double panting and air shots

This problem happens as a result of focusing too much on the techniques. This makes the activity tiring at first but this is something that you will get past through the days. It is only normal that the brain is still not used to the required coordination of the arm and foot movements, and when to squeeze and release the pole. Your mind tends to think harder, especially in the beginning. Practice the techniques until they come out naturally. When you reach this point, your brain will stop from worrying and thinking too much about the technicalities of the activity.

Lessen the load on your mind by doing single arm poling. This way, your mind will think about each alternate action at a time. You can always try the double arm poling when you have gathered enough experience and you already know how to avoid the common pitfalls of the activity.

4. Painful elbows

The correct technique in Nordic walking is having a soft elbow. This means that you will slightly bend your elbow as your arm swings to the front. Avoid the elbow hinge or clamping your upper arm to your side, which causes the elbow joint to work doubly hard. The joint of your elbow is vulnerable and small. It easily absorbs the force that you exert on the pole. If you will continue doing it the wrong way, you will likely end up having a tennis elbow. When you swing your arm, reach as far as you can to the front with your knuckles pointed down. Make sure that the action feels comfortable and does not cause too much strain and pain.

5. Pain in the lower back

When you experience this problem after Nordic walking, it means that your back exerted too much effort during the exercise. To check if you are overworking your back while walking, focus on the muscles of your abdomen. As you push the pole to the ground, the muscles in the stomach must contract automatically. You can try pulling your belly button up as you walk to relieve the pressure from your back.

Practice Makes Perfect

Although it may look easy, Nordic walking requires your full attention. This is actually considered a technical sport with techniques and rules that you have to practice in order to become better.

What will happen if you go about the process without knowing the rules and without being guided properly?

- Your arm swing will work the muscles on your chest, upper arm, and middle back. The movement must be similar to a pendulum with the arm straight and the elbow locked off. If done improperly, your forearm will hurt and you will develop a tennis elbow.

- Is it important to rotate the torso? What will happen if you will skip this part? The action makes your middle back stronger. It eases the tension in your shoulder and neck. It also works on your waist and boosts the flow of oxygen and fluids to your discs, vertebrae, and spine. You will not experience these benefits if you will merely walk with performing this slight rotation of the torso.

- If you often find yourself with a backache after Nordic walking, it may be due to your posture. Make sure that you are always leaning forward. It stabilizes your muscles and helps in improving your balance.
- To boost the blood and oxygen circulation in your system, always pay attention to the hell/toe roll action. The movement of your hands also plays an important role in this regard. Open, close, and squeeze your hand to poles as you walk.

The techniques in Nordic walking also vary depending on where you are walking.

Nordic walking on slopes

It is extremely satisfying to Nordic walk up and down the hill. It is less tiring when going uphill than downhill. Always focus on your posture as you walk through the paths. Make sure that your weight is evenly distributed throughout your body.

1. The uphill technique

Continue doing the heel/toe movement as long as you can. Maintain your proper posture when the slope becomes steep, which might make it hard for you to actively roll your heel and toe. The length of your stride increases when walking along the gentle inclines. The length naturally decreases when you encounter steeper inclines. You can lean into a slope, but avoid misaligning your body to the point of getting injured. Lean from your ankles and do not do the action from your hip. This will misalign your body and put a lot of tension on your lower back.

How do you avoid bending from the hip while actively doing the heel/toe roll? Stand tall as you walk and maintain the proper gaps between your body parts. Swing your arm as naturally as you can. Do not make it tight and avoid clamping the upper portion of the arm to the side of your body. The action will cause your elbow to bend, which will decrease the benefits that you can get from an uphill climb. It is better to use double arm poling on the very steep parts of the slope.

2. The downhill technique

The important thing to remember when Nordic walking downhill is to stabilize your body. It can be achieved by tightening the muscles of your glutes and stomach.

- Bend your knees and soften them. Lower the bend as the slope becomes steeper.
- It is normal for your stride to become shorter. Do not exert effort

in increasing your speed. It is normal at this point to go slower.

- Keep the poles at your back and lean on them. The center of your gravity must be concentrated at the back of your knees in order to take the pressure off from the joint.

- When going downhill, continue walking and skip the action of rotating your torso because this will make you lose your balance.

- Do not lean your body forward as you plant the pole to the ground. Make sure that the pole is planted firmly because it will give you support and ensure your safety. Leaning forward might result to getting pushed off down the hill.

- As you walk down the hill, pay attention to your body. Keep your shoulders down while your body is lifted up.

- It is unavoidable to encounter slippery hills. You can skip the techniques at this instance and put your poles to the front. You can also zigzag down the slope until you are on a part you feel comfortable to continue Nordic walking.

Walking in Muddy Surfaces

Walking in the mud provides a challenging but good workout. It strengthens your arms, core, and legs, as you try your best to keep your stance and avoid sliding and slipping off the ground. The activity tones your muscles and allows you to burn more calories.

This is difficult and advised only for experienced walkers. It can get frustrating when you can't help but slip in many directions as you try your best to push your body to the front. At this instance, keep your focus on your feet and remember the following pointers:

1. Make sure that you are wearing the right footwear. Wear boots with soles that can give enough protection against the sharp objects hidden in the mud. Make sure that the grip of the shoes is comfortable and not too tight. It has to fit perfectly to your feet. If it is too loose, it might come off when you step on a sticky mud. If it is too tight, you won't be able to move your legs properly and your feet will ache after the activity. The boots must be made of durable materials and won't puncture when the sharp ends of the poles hit them.

2. Wear a pair of gaiters to protect your trousers. Most of these materials have a little hook at the bottom. Place the hook at

the front and clip it under your shoe lace. Use the elastic toggle feature of the gaiters to tuck in outside of your leg. This way, you will avoid the spike of the pole from getting caught in the gaiters.

3. The poles work efficiently on muddy surfaces. You can perform heel/toe roll as you actively walk. Always pay attention to how the pole supports the back of your foot as you push forward. At this point, the pole is planted alongside your back foot. You will stabilize your body by pushing the pole firmly. The action will reduce your chances of slipping backward and sideways. As you continue to go forward, engage your core by keeping the gap between the top of your shoulder and your ear lobe as far as you can.

4. Never skip your stretches at the end of each muddy walk. The activity strains your legs and hips because you have placed too much attention on keeping your balance throughout the walk. Start by stretching the outer and inner part of each leg.

Stretch your hip flexors after, followed by the glutes. When you are done with the lower part of your body, perform stretching exercises on your shoulders and neck.

The Basic Heel/Toe Roll

Your foot action is the most important part in this kind of activity. Your speed and how you walk affect the benefits that you can gain from the exercise. Practice the technique even while at home or before you begin with the action. The rolling action of the foot must start from the heel, to the arch of the foot, and then to the ball, before going to the toes. The actions must feel natural and your foot must feel pliable and soft all throughout.

Do not put too much force in each movement of your foot. Avoid pushing off with your toes and slamming down the base of your foot to the ground. Remember the following to get this action done properly:

- Keep your weight evenly distributed over your feet.
- Before pushing off with your toes, make sure that they are widely spread to give your body ample support. The action will open the joint of your ankle, which in effect, will enhance your walking gait. Keep on pushing off with your toes when you feel like you are ready to increase your speed. This will force your body to utilize the gluteal muscles of your buttocks.
- When you lift your toe, always use the strength coming from the shin

muscle. This is also a common problem done by many Nordic walkers that result to developing a shuffling walking pattern when you get older and a weak shin muscle.

Conclusion

Thank you again for purchasing this book!

I hope this book was able to help you to understand the benefits of Nordic walking and how easy it is to begin with it.

The next step is to buy your gears, shop for the right outfit depending on the weather and make sure that they fit, find the right people whom you can tag along, and make this a part of your long-term health regime.

Printed in Great Britain
by Amazon